Black
Achievement
IN SCIENCE
Medicine

MC

Mason Crest

Black
Achievement
IN SCIENCE

Biology	Inventors
Chemistry	Medicine
Computer Science	Physics
Engineering	Space
Environmental Science	Technology

Black
Achievement
IN SCIENCE

Medicine

By MARI RICH

Foreword by Malinda Gilmore and Mel Poulson,
National Organization for the Advancement of
Black Chemists and Chemical Engineers

Mason Crest
450 Parkway Drive, Suite D
Broomall, PA 19008
www.masoncrest.com

Printed and bound in the United States of America.

Series ISBN: 978-1-4222-3554-6
Hardback ISBN: 978-1-4222-3561-4
EBook ISBN: 978-1-4222-8328-8

First printing
1 3 5 7 9 8 6 4 2

Produced by Shoreline Publishing Group LLC
Santa Barbara, California
Editorial Director: James Buckley Jr.
Designer: Patty Kelley
Production: Sandy Gordon
www.shorelinepublishing.com
Cover photograph by Nanditha Rao/Dreamstime.

Library of Congress Cataloging-in-Publication Data

Names: Rich, Mari.
Title: Medicine / by Mari Rich ; foreword, by Malinda Gilmore and Mel Poulson, National Organization for the Advancement of Black Chemists and Chemical Engineers.
Description: Broomall, PA : Mason Crest, [2017] | Includes index.
Identifiers: LCCN 2016002451| ISBN 9781422235614 (hardback) | ISBN 9781422235546 (series) | ISBN 9781422283288 (ebook)
Subjects: LCSH: African American physicians--Biography--Juvenile literature. | Physicians--United States--Biography--Juvenile literature. | Women   physicians--United States--Biography--Juvenile literature.
Classification: LCC R153 .R53 2017 | DDC 610.92/273--dc23
LC record available at http://lccn.loc.gov/2016002451

Contents

Key Icons to Look for

 Words to Understand: These words with their easy-to-understand definitions will increase the reader's understanding of the text, while building vocabulary skills.

 Research Projects: Readers are pointed toward areas of further inquiry connected to each chapter. Suggestions are provided for projects that encourage deeper research and analysis.

 Text-Dependent Questions: These questions send the reader back to the text for more careful attention to the evidence presented here.

 Series Glossary of Key Terms: This back-of-the-book glossary contains terminology used throughout this series. Words found here increase the reader's ability to read and comprehend higher-level books and articles in this field.

 Educational Videos: Readers can view videos by scanning our QR codes, providing them with additional educational content to supplement the text. Examples include news coverage, moments in history, speeches, iconic moments, and much more!

Science, Technology, Engineering and Mathematics (STEM) are vital to our future, the future of our country, the future of our regions, and the future of our children. STEM is everywhere and it shapes our everyday experiences. Science and technology have become the leading foundation of global development. Both subjects continue to improve the quality of life as new findings, inventions, and creations emerge from the basis of science. A career in a STEM discipline is a fantastic choice and one that should be explored by many.

In today's society, STEM is becoming more diverse and even internationalized. However, the shortage of African Americans and other minorities, including women, still exists. This series—*Black Achievement in Science*—reveals the numerous career choices and pathways that great African-American scientists, technologists, engineers, and mathematicians have pursued to become successful in a STEM discipline. The purpose of this series of books is to inspire, motivate, encourage, and educate people about the numerous career choices and pathways in STEM. We applaud the authors for sharing the experiences of our forefathers and foremothers and ultimately increasing the number of people of color in STEM and, more

By Malinda Gilmore, NOBCChE Executive Board Chair and Mel Poulson, NOBCChE Executive Board Vice-Chair specifically, increasing the number of African Americans to pursue careers in STEM.

The personal experiences and accomplishments shared within are truly inspiring and gratifying. It is our hope that by reading about the lives and careers of these great scientists, technologists, engineers, and mathematicians, the reader might become inspired and totally committed to pursue a career in a STEM discipline and say to themselves, "If they were able to do it, then I am definitely able to do it, and this, too, can be me." Hopefully, the reader will realize that these great accomplishments didn't come easily. It was because of hard work, perseverance, and determination that these chosen individuals were so successful.

As Executive Board Members of The National Organization for the Professional Advancement of Black Chemists and Chemical Engineers (NOBCChE) we are excited about this series. For more than 40 years, NOBCChE has promoted the STEM fields and its mission is to build an eminent cadre of people of color in STEM. Our mission is in line with the overall purpose of this series and we are indeed committed to inspiring our youth to explore and contribute to our country's future in science, technology, engineering, and mathematics.

We encourage all readers to enjoy the series in its entirety and identify with a personal story that resonates well with you. Learn more about that person and their career pathway, and you can be just like them.

The statistics are troubling: African-American men are more than twice as likely to die of prostate cancer as their white counterparts, and black women almost twice as likely to succumb to breast cancer as women of other races. The mortality rate for black infants is twice that of whites, and blacks, on the whole, are several times more likely than whites to suffer from high blood pressure and diabetes.

Some experts think that in addition to the obvious reasons—such as higher poverty levels, lack of insurance, and reduced access to nutritious food choices in black communities—a major culprit might be a shortage of black medical personnel. They point out that surveys have shown that black patients tend to feel more comfortable with black doctors and are more likely to seek needed treatment if they have access to a physician of color. (Geography also becomes a factor; black doctors are more likely to set up their offices in low-income areas, where choices for medical care are few and far between.)

While it seems that the easy answer would be to train greater numbers of black doctors, the path to medical school has not traditionally been an easy one for aspiring, young people of color. The very first African-American man to earn a medical degree, James McCune Smith (1813-1865), had to travel to Europe to do so. The situation improved only gradually.

In 1868, the College of Medicine at the historically black Howard University opened in Washington, D.C., and in

1876 Meharry Medical College, in Nashville, Tennessee, was established to train black physicians. Even when those institutions began graduating students, however, young black M.D.s found it difficult to get further training that would allow them to practice vitally needed medical specialties. Also, few white hospitals would allow them to see patients.

With the the Civil Rights Movement in the 1960s and the push for integration, blacks began gaining access to white medical schools and hospitals, but they continued to face racism and prejudice. Although attitudes have arguably become more enlightened in the ensuing

Careers in health care fields are expected to grow in the near future.

decades, there is still a shortage of black physicians: according to recent census data, African Americans account for approximately 14 percent of the population, but they represent just five percent of all practicing doctors.

The towering figures in this volume—whether they hail from the 19th century or our own era—should serve as inspiration for a new generation of medical students. Read more about the steps needed to join their ranks in the final chapter. The statistics make it clear that disease and mortality are not colorblind, and increasing the number of minority physicians will greatly improve the chances that patients of color get access to much-needed, quality healthcare. ●

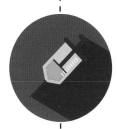

Words to Understand

druggist
another term for pharmacist, a professional who dispenses prescription and other medicine

remuneration
pay or salary for work

Chapter 1

Rebecca Davis (Lee) Crumpler

Born: 1831

Died: 1895

Nationality: American

Achievements: First African–American woman doctor; author of important early medical text.

R ebecca Davis Lee Crumpler was the first African-American woman ever to become a medical doctor, and the volume she published in 1883, *A Book of Medical Discourses*, is widely acknowledged as being among the first medical texts ever written by a black person.

The future physician was born Rebecca Davis Lee on February 8, 1831, in Delaware. Her parents were Matilda Webber and Absolum Davis. She was raised for the most part by an aunt in Pennsylvania who was often called upon to care for ill neighbors. (Poor blacks typically had no access to professionally trained medical personnel in that era.)

The introduction to *A Book of Medical Discourses*, which is available in the digital collection of the US National Library of Medicine, informs readers: "It may be well to state here that, having been reared by a kind

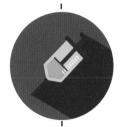

aunt in Pennsylvania, whose usefulness with the sick was continually sought, I early conceived a liking for, and sought every opportunity to relieve the sufferings of others."

By 1852, the young woman had moved to Massachusetts, where she worked as a nurse. She wrote of this period in her book, "Later in life I devoted my time, when best I could, to nursing as a business, serving under different doctors for a period of eight years (from 1852 to 1860), most of the time at my adopted home in Charlestown, Middlesex County, Massachusetts. From these doctors I received letters commending me to the faculty of the New England Female Medical College, whence, four years afterward, I received the degree of doctress of medicine." It was highly unusual for even a black man to be admitted to medical school—a fact that makes apparent the high level of skill she must have demonstrated as a self-taught nurse.

As a medical student, she had few role models: of the more than 54,000 doctors working in the U.S. in 1860, only about 300 were women, and of those women, none were black. Her academic career did not always go smoothly. She had been at the medical college for only a year when the Civil War broke out, interrupting her studies. Then, she returned in 1863, only to find out that her financial aid was no longer available, Benjamin Wade, an abolitionist from Ohio, heard of her plight and provided her with a scholarship, allowing her to complete her studies in 1864. At about the time of her graduation, she married a man named Arthur Crumpler, whom many sources refer to as a fellow doctor.

After the Civil War ended in 1865—realizing that there would be many newly freed slaves requiring medical care—Crumpler moved to the South. She wrote, "After the close of the Confederate War, my mind centered on Richmond, the capital city of Virginia, as the proper field for real missionary work, and one that would present ample opportunities to become acquainted with the diseases of women and children."

Her prediction proved correct. As she wrote, "During my stay there nearly every hour was improved in that sphere of labor. The last quarter of the year 1866, I was enabled … to have access each day to a very large number of the indigent, and others of different classes, in a population of over 30,000 colored."

Crumpler worked in Richmond for the Bureau of Refugees, Freedmen, and Abandoned Lands (more generally known as the Freedmen's Bureau), a U.S. government agency established in 1865 to aid freed slaves during the Reconstruction Era and to change attitudes in the former Confederacy. Those attitudes were slow to change, however. Crumpler frequently found herself the target

Surgeons and doctors learned a great deal about injuries and trauma during the Civil War.

of blatant sexism and racism—with male doctors refusing to work with her, **druggists** reluctant to fill prescriptions she had written, and the more blatant among them asserting that her M.D. stood for "mule driver."

In 1869, Crumpler and her husband moved back to Boston. After her experiences in Richmond, she wrote, "I entered into the work with renewed vigor, practicing outside, and receiving children in the house for treatment; regardless, in a measure, of **remuneration**."

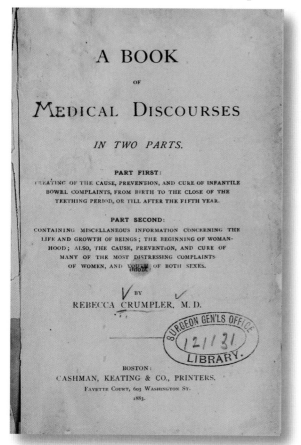

Crumpler called on her long career as a medical professional to write her book.

Crumpler and her husband moved to Hyde Park, Massachusetts, in 1889, and shortly thereafter she retired from the active practice of medicine. That is when she used her notes to write *A Book of Medical Discourses*.

Crumpler died on March 9, 1895. In 1989 two female physicians, Saundra Maass-Robinson and Patricia Whitley, founded a professional organization, the Rebecca Lee Society, in her honor. Additionally, the

Association of Black Women Physicians awards a scholarship in her name.

Nowhere in her book, which is the primary source of information on her life, does Crumpler acknowledge her status as the nation's first female African-American physician. As a result, historians had long credited Rebecca Cole, an 1867 graduate of the Women's Medical College of Pennsylvania, with that role. As important as Dr. Cole was, Dr. R.L. Crumpler came first. ●

Rebecca Lee Crumpler:
Early American doctor

Words to Understand

pericardium
the sac of fibrous tissue that surrounds the heart

recuperate
over time, recover from an illness or surgery

Daniel Hale Williams

Born:
1856

Died:
1931

Natinality:
American

Achievements:
Pioneering surgeon and hospital founder; performed first open-heart surgery

D aniel Hale Williams has a long list of accomplishments to his credit. He founded the first medical facility in the US to have an interracial staff; helped start the National Medical Association, a professional organization for blacks, as an alternative to the American Medical Association, which didn't allow them to join; and was among the first doctors ever to perform successful open-heart surgery.

Williams was born on January 18, 1856, in Hollidaysburg, Pennsylvania. He was one of eight children born to Sarah (Price) Williams and Daniel Hale Williams II, a barber who was an avid member of the National Equal Rights League, an organization launched during the Civil War.

When Williams was about ten years old, his father died of tuberculosis. Williams was

apprenticed to a shoemaker during his teens but found that he did not enjoy the work and pursued barbering, like his late father, instead.

Wanting to pursue higher education, he attended high school (which was unusual enough for African Americans of that era), and then entered a post-secondary academy, where he remained until the age of 21. Deciding to pursue a career in medicine, Williams, who had relocated to Wisconsin by then, became an apprentice under Henry Palmer, a prominent area surgeon. Thanks to his experience with Palmer, Williams was accepted in 1880 to a three-year program at the Chicago Medical School, which was affiliated with Northwestern University. There, in 1883, he earned an M.D. degree.

That year, there were only a handful of black doctors in Chicago, and Williams joined their ranks. He worked at a facility called the South Side Dispensary, where he practiced general medicine and

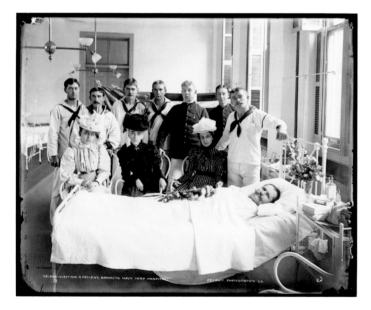

Hospitals of the late 1800s were primitive by today's standards, but even worse for most black patients.

performed surgery. He had contracts with the City Railway Company and the Protestant Orphan Asylum and became known not just for his competence but his willingness to treat both black and white patients. In 1889, Williams was appointed to the Illinois State Board of Health, where he became acutely aware of how poorly black patients were treated in many hospitals.

Williams opened the Provident Hospital as the first integrated medical school.

In 1890, Louis Reynolds, a local pastor, told Williams the story of his sister Emma, who wanted to be a nurse but was repeatedly refused admission to nursing schools because she was black. Determined to do more than merely sympathize, on May 4, 1891, he opened the Provident Hospital and Nursing Training School, the country's first such medical facility to be racially integrated.

In its first year of operation, Provident treated almost 200 patients, over 85 percent of whom enjoyed a full recovery. That rate was considered exceptional, given the poverty and horrendous health of most of the patients. Much of Provident's success was attributed to Williams and his insistence on cleanliness and cutting-edge sanitation procedures.

One July day in 1893, a young man named James Cornish was brought to Provident suffering from deep knife wounds to his chest and quickly going into shock. As six

doctors—some white and some black—crowded the operating room to observe, Williams cut Cornish's rib cartilage, getting access to the heart. He discovered a badly damaged artery and confidently sutured it, but then, examining the **pericardium**, he realized that the knife had left a large gash near another artery. With the heart still beating—and few other options—Williams rinsed the wound with a salt solution and painstakingly sewed the edges together. Cornish remained at Provident to **recuperate** for 51 days and lived for more than two decades after that. That seemingly miraculous operation has been widely hailed as one of the first open-heart surgeries ever performed, with many sources referring to it as the very first.

In 1894, Williams became chief surgeon at Freedmen's Hospital, in Washington, D.C., where he oversaw a large decline in the facility's mortality rate, started an ambulance service, increased the number of doctors certified in specialties, and made other improvements. In 1898, after his marriage to a teacher, he returned to Provident to serve as chief surgeon, and he also established a thriving private practice.

Williams remains a hero to doctors of all backgrounds.

In 1900, he became a visiting professor of surgery at Meharry Medical College in Nashville, Tennessee, then one of only two black medical schools in the country. In 1912, he resigned from Provident to accept a post as attending staff surgeon at St. Luke's Hospital in Chicago.

Williams—who in 1913 became the first African American to be inducted into the American College of Surgeons—practiced medicine until 1926, when he suffered a stroke. At the time of his death, in 1931, he was living in Michigan.

Throughout his career, Williams was known to his staff and grateful patients as "Dr. Dan", and some sources report that at the Howard University Hospital, a "code blue," the widely used signal that a patient is in need of resuscitation, is instead called a "Dr. Dan." ●

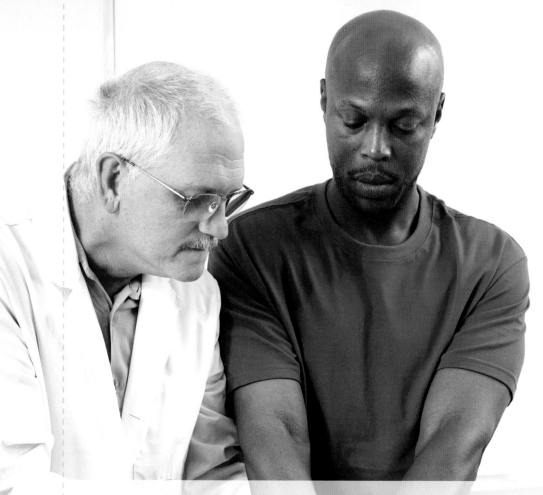

Words to Understand

bacteriology
the study of bacteria, especially those one-celled organisms that are involved in infectious diseases

immunology
a science that deals with the ways in which the body protects itself from diseases and infections

physiology
the branch of biology dealing with the functions and activities of living organisms

serological
related to serology, a medical science dealing with blood serum, its reactions, and its properties

Chapter 3

William Hinton

Born:
1883

Died:
1959

Nationality:
American

Achievements:
Educator, author, and creator of groundbreaking test for syphilis

William Augustus Hinton has the distinction of being both the first black professor ever to teach at Harvard Medical School and the first black physician ever to publish a widely used textbook. A pioneering figure in the field of public health, he is perhaps most widely celebrated as the developer of a highly accurate **serological** test for syphilis, a potentially life-threatening bacterial infection usually spread by sexual contact.

Hinton was born on December 15, 1883, in Chicago, Illinois. His parents, Augustus and Maria, were former slaves who had been freed after the Civil War. The family settled in Kansas, where Hinton excelled academically, thanks in large measure to the encouragement of his parents, who were eager to see him enjoy greater financial stability and social respect than had been accorded to them.

Hinton attended the University of Kansas for two years before transferring to Harvard, where he earned a B.S. degree in 1905. Although he wanted to become a doctor, with little money for tuition he instead accepted teaching posts at various schools in Oklahoma and Tennessee. During the summers, he arranged to study at the University of Chicago, where he focused on **bacteriology** and **physiology**.

Finally, in 1909 he was able to enroll in Harvard Medical School. While the esteemed institution initially offered him a scholarship for black students, Hinton declined that honor. He chose to compete with all students for two prestigious prizes, both of which he won.

After earning his medical degree with honors in 1912, Hinton remained at the school to work in its Wassermann Lab, where he taught serology. When Wassermann became the official lab of the Massachusetts State Department of Public Health in 1915, Hinton was put in charge of that facility and also named assistant director of the state's Division of Biologic Laboratories. During this period as head of the Boston Dispensary's laboratory department, he created a program to train female lab technicians.

In 1918, Hinton began teaching preventive medicine and hygiene at the Harvard Medical School, and he later added courses in bacteriology and **immunology**, ultimately teaching those subjects to three decades of Harvard medical students.

Concurrently, Hinton continued his duties at Wassermann, where he developed a highly accurate test for syphilis that was endorsed by the US Public Health Service in 1934. The test was simple to administer, cost-effective, and quick, and came to be called simply the Hinton Test.

In 1936, Hinton published *Syphilis and Its Treatment*, generally considered the first medical textbook by a black American. Two years later the National Association for the Advancement of Colored People (NAACP) expressed its intention to give Hinton the Spingarn Medal for outstanding achievement. As he had done with Harvard's race-based scholarship, he turned the organization down.

Hinton spent most of his career on the faculty of Harvard Medical School.

Hinton, who lost a leg in an auto accident in 1940, retired from Harvard in 1950, gaining the title of professor emeritus. He practiced for a time at a Massachusetts hospital for disabled children, but in 1953 he was forced to retire completely because of his diabetes and rapidly failing eyesight. By then, the Wassermann Lab was testing some 2,000 specimens for syphilis every day.

Hinton died on August 8, 1959. In his will, he left $75,000 to Harvard to establish a scholarship fund for graduate students. He instructed that it be called the Dwight D. Eisenhower Scholarship Fund, to honor a president he admired for his dedication to equal-opportunity employment. ●

Words to Understand

coagulation
the process by which blood clots to form solid masses

neuroanatomy
the study of the structure and function of the brain and other components of the nervous system

plasma
the liquid in which the blood cells are suspended

transfusion
the transfer of blood (or a component of blood) from one person to another to replace losses caused by injury, surgery, or disease

Chapter 4

Charles Richard Drew

Born:
1904

Died:
1950

Nationality:
American

Achievements:
Created first way to process
and store blood plasma,
saving millions of lives

Some historians date the first-ever successful blood **transfusion** back to 1667, when doctors in France transfused the blood of a sheep into a desperately ill fifteen-year-old boy, who survived the procedure. The year 1818 marked the first recorded human-to-human procedure, when a British obstetrician injected a patient who was bleeding internally with a pint of blood gathered from several donors. (That patient died soon after.)

It was not until physician Charles Richard Drew developed a way to process, preserve, and store blood **plasma** during World War II, however, that large-scale blood banks as they exist today were made possible.

Drew was born on June 3, 1904, in Washington, D.C. His father, Richard, worked as a carpet layer, and his mother, Nora, taught school. As a young man, Drew was gifted

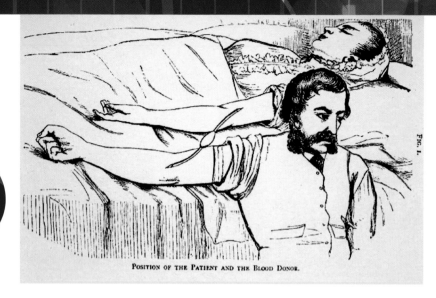

POSITION OF THE PATIENT AND THE BLOOD DONOR.

The idea of blood transfusions had been around for centuries, but until Drew solved the storage problem, all transfusions were direct.

both academically and athletically. While in elementary school, he was a star member of the swim team, and later he also played football and basketball. He attended Paul Laurence Dunbar High School, which had been established shortly after the Civil War and was originally called the Preparatory High School for Colored Youth; so stellar was the school's reputation that black parents often moved to the area so that their children could attend.

Drew excelled at Dunbar, and after graduating in 1922 he was awarded a sports scholarship to Amherst College, where he became a valued member of the track and football teams. He earned his bachelor's degree four years later.

Drew long wanted to attend medical school, but with little money for tuition, he instead took a job as biology instructor and athletic coach at Baltimore's Morgan College, now called Morgan State University. In 1928 he enrolled at McGill University, in Montreal, Canada. As in both high school and college, he excelled, winning a prize in **neuroanatomy**.

Drew graduated as salutatorian in 1933, earning both Doctor of Medicine and Master of Surgery degrees. It was during his internship and residency at the Royal Victoria Hospital and Montreal General that he became particularly interested in the topic of blood transfusions.

In 1935, Drew returned to the United States and accepted a post as a pathology instructor at Howard University's medical school. Then, in 1938 he received a fellowship to study and work at Columbia University and its affiliated Presbyterian Hospital, in New York City.

At Columbia, where he worked under the direction of Dr. John Scudder, Drew continued his research on blood transfusion. Before 1914, blood had to be transfused immediately after being drawn from a donor to prevent **coagulation**, but then physicians realized that adding a chemical called sodium citrate effectively kept it from clotting. Refrigerating the sodium citrate-treated blood then made it possible to store it for a few days.

Drew discovered that plasma could be dried and then reconstituted only when needed, making for relatively easy long-term storage and transport. (He also realized that since blood cells determine blood type, plasma—which contains no blood cells—could be given to anyone regardless of their blood type.) He and Scudder subsequently set up a trial blood bank at Presbyterian, learning to deal with a formidable list of challenges. Drew wrote his doctoral thesis, *Banked Blood*, on the basis of that work and was awarded his doctoral degree in medical science in 1940.

Plasma, because it contains vital proteins and antibodies that can help stabilize blood pressure and regulate clotting, can be particularly useful in battlefield situations, and as World War II spread throughout Europe, in June 1940 Drew was put in charge of a medical program called Blood for Britain. In that capacity he collected and processed plasma from several New York hospitals and arranged for it to be shipped overseas. By the time the program ended, in January 1941, Drew had helped send some 14,500 pints of plasma to England.

In early 1941, Drew began helping the American Red Cross develop a blood bank program for the U.S. military. Initially, the military requested that no black donors be accepted; they later relented and agreed to accept blood from African Americans—with the proviso that it be given only to African-American servicemen. The policy naturally angered and frustrated Drew, who resigned within months.

While still in New York City, he sat for and passed the American Board of Surgery exams. In mid-1941 he became the first African-American examiner the American Board of Surgery had ever appointed.

Upon leaving New York, Drew returned to Howard University, where he

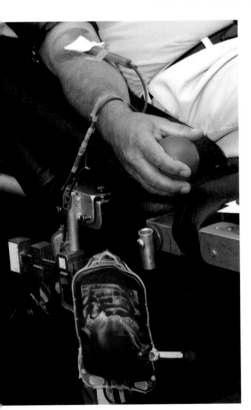

Millions of people donate blood products each year.

was appointed Chairman of the Department of Surgery and Chief of Surgery at Freedmen's Hospital, Howard's main teaching facility. He trained more than half of the nation's black surgeons, and his students often achieved the top scores. Despite these achievements, Drew never gained admission to the American Medical Association. As a black physician he was excluded from joining the local District of Columbia chapter of the group.

Drew, who garnered the National Association for the Advancement of Colored People's 1943 Spingarn Medal for "highest and noblest achievement," was killed in a car crash on April 1, 1950, on his way back from a medical conference at the Tuskegee Institute in Alabama.

He has since been awarded numerous posthumous honors. He was featured, for example, in the U.S. Postal Service's "Great Americans" stamp series in 1981, and the Charles R. Drew University of Medicine and Science, a private, nonprofit institution in South Los Angeles that educates many minority students, was named in his honor. ●

Charles Richard Drew:
Master of blood transfusion

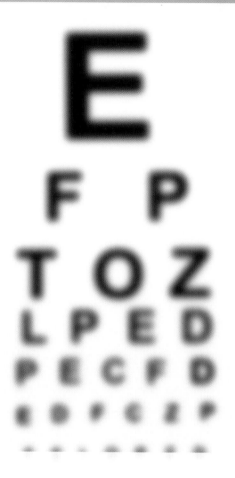

Words to Understand

cataract
a medical condition in which the lens of the eye becomes increasingly cloudy, resulting in blurred vision

irrigation
in medicine, flooding a wound or incision with liquid

ophthalmic
having to do with vision science

ophthalmology
a branch of medical science dealing with the structure, functions, and diseases of the eye

Chapter 5

Patricia Bath

Born:
1942

Nationality:
American

Achievements:
Opthamologist and inventor
who created a new
instrument to treat
eye problems

Patricia Bath has been widely celebrated as the first African-American person ever to complete a medical residency in **ophthalmology** and the first African-American female doctor to receive a medical patent. She earned the latter in 1988 for the Laserphaco Probe, an invention that led to advancements in **cataract** treatment. She is also applauded for her belief that "eyesight is a basic human right" and for her efforts to promote "community ophthalmology," volunteer-based outreach efforts to bring much-needed eye care to those who might not otherwise have access to it.

Bath was born on November 4, 1942, in the predominately black New York City neighborhood of Harlem. Her father, Rupert, an immigrant from Trinidad, worked at a variety of jobs, including merchant seaman.

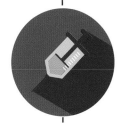

He had the distinction of being the first black motorman ever hired to work on the New York City subway system. Bath's mother, Gladys, sometimes worked as a maid, and she banked her earnings to pay for Bath's future college tuition. Education was a priority for the couple. Rupert, who had traveled widely as a seaman, stressed the importance of learning about other cultures, and Gladys delighted in buying Bath chemistry sets, microscopes, and books on science.

When Bath was sixteen and a student at Charles Evan Hughes High School, she took part in a highly selective program funded by the National Science Foundation that allowed her to do biomedical research at Yeshiva University in New York. There she worked on a project that examined the relationship between cancer, nutrition, and stress. In 1960, she presented her findings at a national medical conference and was recognized by the editors of *Mademoiselle* magazine for her contributions to science.

Bath graduated from high school in under three years, and she next entered Hunter College, part of the public City University of New York system. After earning a bachelor's degree in chemistry in 1964, she attended the medical school at Howard University, a historically black school where she studied for the first time with African-American professors.

While at Howard, Bath received a National Institute of Health fellowship and the Edwin J. Watson Prize for Outstanding Student in Ophthalmology, among other honors. Inspired by the humanitarian work of Dr. Albert Schweitzer, she also spent one summer in Yugoslavia, studying children's health, and she helped organize a social-justice march on Washington, D.C. Bath earned her medical degree in 1968 and returned to New York City, where she worked as an intern at Harlem Hospital and accepted an ophthalmology fellowship at Columbia University.

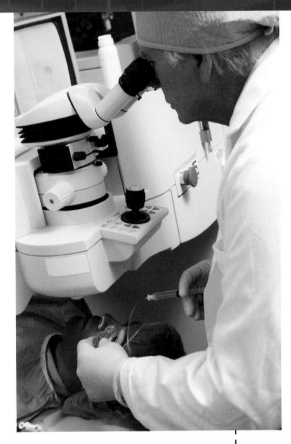

Eye surgeons use lasers and high-powered lenses to do delicate eye procedures.

She was distressed to realize that the black patients at Harlem Hospital had more severe vision problems than their white counterparts at Columbia University. Formally researching the issue, she discovered that blindness was twice as common among African Americans because they had less access to quality **ophthalmic** care. In response, she called upon her colleagues at Columbia to lend their services free of charge at Harlem Hospital's Eye Clinic. Because of this, she is widely credited with pioneering the concept of community ophthalmology, which combines public health, community service, and ophthalmology to treat needy populations.

In 1973 Bath, who was by then affiliated with New York University, became the first African American of either gen-

der to complete a residency in ophthalmology. After a year of working as an assistant surgeon at small New York hospitals, she moved to the West Coast to become an assistant professor of surgery at the Charles R. Drew University and the University of California, Los Angeles (UCLA). She was the first African–American woman surgeon at UCLA's Medical Center, and in 1975 she became the first female faculty member in the Department of Ophthalmology at UCLA's Jules Stein Eye Institute.

In 1976, Bath co-founded the American Institute for the Prevention of Blindness (AIPB), which was dedicated to the premise that "eyesight is a basic human right." In that capacity, she traveled to Nigeria to work as a visiting chief of ophthalmology and served as an advisor to the White House Counsel on its National and International Blindness Prevention Program.

Despite her many other accomplishments, Bath is perhaps best known for being the first black, female doctor to patent a medical device: the Laserphaco Probe, which consisted of an optical laser surrounded by tiny tubes for suction and **irrigation**. Bath had learned about laser surgery while in Germany and realized that the technology might

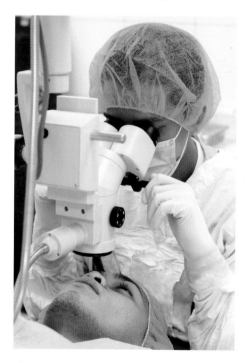

Bath has focused most of her career on making sure that everyone has access to high-quality vision care.

allow for the more efficient and less painful removal of cataracts.

Previously, cataracts were removed laboriously by hand, using a mechanical grinding device. By contrast, surgeons could insert Bath's laser probe, which had taken her some five years to develop, into a one-millimeter incision in the eye. The laser vaporized the affected lens, which was then washed from the eye via the tubes before a replacement lens was inserted. The procedure was easier, more precise, and more comfortable than previous methods, and is now used all over the world. Bath herself has reportedly restored the vision of patients who had been blind for decades using the technology, and she has since been awarded three additional patents, for improvements to the original device.

Although Bath retired from UCLA in 1993, she continues to preside over the AIPB, and her goal is to eradicate preventable blindness worldwide by 2020. ●

Patricia Bath:
Saving eyes and vision

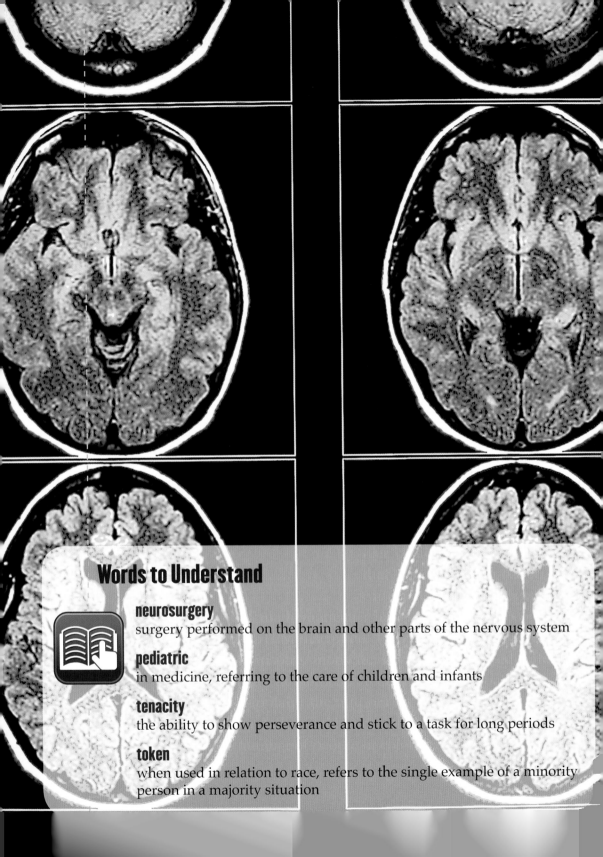

Words to Understand

neurosurgery
surgery performed on the brain and other parts of the nervous system

pediatric
in medicine, referring to the care of children and infants

tenacity
the ability to show perseverance and stick to a task for long periods

token
when used in relation to race, refers to the single example of a minority person in a majority situation

Chapter 6

Alexa Canady

Born:
1950

Nationality:
American

Achievements:
First African–American
woman neurosurgeon;
known for her work
with children

Alexa Canady was the first black woman in the nation ever to specialize in **neurosurgery**, which she has referred to as "the most intensely male [dominated] of all the medical specialties." In an era when few women even attempted to earn medical degrees, Canady found that being black gave her a distinct, if ironic, advantage. "Professors frequently overlooked the women's raised hands, and most of the prestigious clubs and societies were all-male," she wrote in an essay posted on the website of the National Women's Law Center. "The white women in my class were shocked and outraged that they weren't being taken seriously. I'd hear them complain between classes about how unfair it was. It was the first time they had felt pushed aside. But I just put my head down and worked harder. I was used to being disregarded."

Canady was born on November 7, 1950, in Lansing, Michigan. Her mother, Elizabeth, had the distinction of being the first African-American person ever elected to the Lansing Board of Education, and her father, Clinton, was a dentist. Canady and her brother were the only two black students in their entire school, and she has recalled one particularly egregious instance of racism on the part of a teacher. The summer before she entered third grade, Canady volunteered at a local college whose psychology students needed test subjects. She scored so well that the professor pronounced her intelligence "off the charts," much to the bewilderment of her parents, who had been told by the school district that she was merely average. Upon investigation, they discovered that Canady's second-grade teacher had lied about the results of that year's tests, assigning Canady's stellar scores to a white classmate rather than admitting that a black child had excelled to such an extent.

Still, her parents did not allow Canady and her brother to be bothered by bigoted attitudes. In her essay, Canady recalled Elizabeth's words: "She said, 'Let them make you the token—so what if you're the **token** black girl. Take that token and spend it.' My mother taught me not to care what other people thought."

Canady entered the University of Michigan, following in her mother's footsteps by majoring in zoology and pledging Delta Sigma Theta, a sorority of African-American women. (Later in life, Elizabeth served as national president of the organization.)

While still an under-graduate, Canady attend-ed a summer program for minority students that allowed her to explore medical careers, and, she enrolled in the University of Michigan's School of Medicine after earning her bachelor's degree in 1971. There she became interested in neurology, the study of the brain and

Canady overcame challenges when a student at the University of Michigan.

nervous system. She was fascinated by the structure of the human brain, which she considered the most complex and mysterious organ in the body, and that soon led her to con-sider the field of neurosurgery. That posed something of a problem, as she wrote, "There were a very limited number of women surgeons at that time, and only a handful in neu-rosurgery," she explained. "As a black woman, how was I going to get into a residency program—in a field in which schools only admit one or two residents a year?" Realiz-ing that her good grades would not be enough to make her stand out, she went on the offensive. "I became a neurosur-gery groupie," she wrote. "I inhaled every publication and article I could get my hands on, and I attended every con-ference and seminar. I went to meetings and asked ques-tions just to make myself known."

Canady was excited to win an interview with the chairman of neurosurgery at Michigan but felt demoralized when he spent the time listing names of former residents whom he had fired. The purpose of the interview, she surmised, was merely to intimidate and dissuade her. Undaunted, however, she broadened her search, traveling around the country to interviews. Her **tenacity** paid off in 1975, when she was granted a residency in general surgery at the Yale-New Haven Hospital. On her first day there, she recalled her mother's "token" speech, and remained calm when a white hospital administrator walked past her muttering, "There's our new equal-opportunity package."

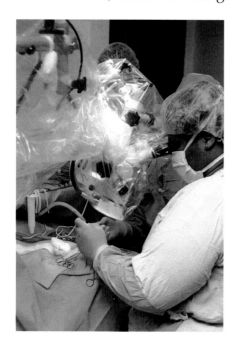

Canady at work is a picture of calm professionalism in one of medicine's toughest jobs.

In 1976, Canady moved to the University of Minnesota's Department of Neurosurgery, becoming the first female African-American neurosurgery resident in the United States. Upon completing her residency in 1981, she thus became the country's first female African-American neurosurgeon. Choosing to specialize as a **pediatric** neurosurgeon, she trained at the Children's Hospital of Philadelphia. She also worked for a time at Detroit's Henry Ford Hospital before becoming chief of neurosurgery at the Children's Hospital of Michigan.

Canady was well known not only for her expertise in a wide variety of brain diseases, but also for the genuine affection she felt for those she treated. "What stands out in my memory are the special relationships I had with my young patients," she wrote. "[They] taught me so much—about living in the moment with tremendous courage and grace despite serious and often terminal illnesses. I took care of some children for 15 to 20 years. I watched them grow up. I got up in the middle of the night to care for them. I cared for every single one of them as if they were my own."

Canady was inducted into the Michigan Women's Hall of Fame and presented with the American Medical Women's Association President's Award. She retired in 2001 and moved to Florida. Her retirement was short-lived, however; when she discovered that there were no pediatric neurosurgeons working in the immediate area, she agreed to see patients part-time at Pensacola's Sacred Heart Hospital. ●

Alexa Canady:
Pioeneering neurosurgeon

Words to Understand

occipital craniopagus twins
conjoined twins (formerly known as Siamese twins) who are born
joined at the occipital lobe in the back of the head

Chapter 7

Ben Carson

Born:
1951

Nationality:
American

Achievements:
Brain surgeon who
performed history-making
operation on
conjoined twin

While some people today know Ben Carson primarily as an outspoken conservative and Republican presidential candidate, before entering the political realm, he had a long, distinguished career as a neurosurgeon. He was known for taking on cases no other doctor would tackle and for performing the world's first successful separation of **occipital craniopagus twins**. Later, he was equally celebrated for his separation of twins fused at the top of the head in an operation that lasted more than 24 hours and marked the first time such conjoined twins had survived the procedure with both being neurologically normal.

Benjamin Solomon Carson was born in Detroit, Michigan, on September 18, 1951, to Sonya Carson, who had been raised in a succession of foster homes in rural Tennessee, and Robert Solomon Carson. Sonya had dropped

out of school in the third grade, and at age thirteen married the much-older Robert. In addition to Ben, their second-born, the couple had another son, Curtis, who is now a mechanical engineer.

Although many successful people got their start in inner-city Detroit, Carson's childhood had an additional twist; Robert had an entire second family that he hid so well that Sonya did not discover that fact until Curtis was ten years old and Ben was eight. The couple subsequently divorced, and Sonya began working two and three jobs at a time, often as a maid, to make ends meet. There were often periods when she left for work at 5:00 in the morning and did not return home until almost midnight.

Devastated by his father's betrayal, Carson, although bright, began failing classes, and he developed a violent temper. He has credited two factors with turning him from his self-destructive path. First, he began reading the Bible and was particularly moved by the Book of Proverbs, where he found a passage that read, "Better a patient man than a warrior, a man who controls his temper than one who takes a city." Sonya was also a major influence, severely limiting his television time and making him read two library books a week. Although she was virtually illiterate herself, she made him prepare written reports on what he had read and would pretend to review them, placing a check at the top of each page to encourage him.

Carson gradually came to enjoy reading and began devouring books of all types—particularly those about scientists. He realized he wanted to pursue a medical career and buckled down to study.

Carson ultimately graduated from Detroit's Southwestern High School with honors and won a scholarship—which he supplemented with earn-

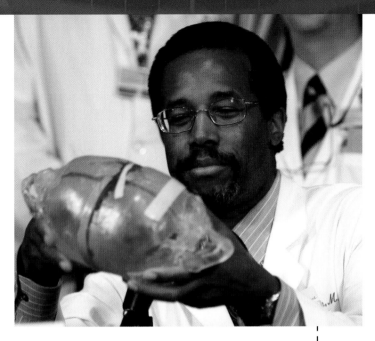

Before the historic operation, Carson used a model to show reporters his techniques.

ings from odd jobs—to Yale University. In 1973, he earned a bachelor's degree in psychology and entered the University of Michigan's School of Medicine. In 1977, he became a resident at the world-renowned Johns Hopkins University, and by 1982 he was the chief resident in neurosurgery there—a feat he attributes to his exceptional eye-hand coordination and ability to visualize the brain in three dimensions.

In 1983, Carson spent a year at the Sir Charles Gairdner Hospital in Perth, Australia. Because Australia had a severe shortage of trained neurosurgeons at the time, Carson credits his short time there with giving him several years' worth of experience. He returned to Johns Hopkins in 1984, and the following year he was made director of pediatric neurosurgery. At 33 years old, he was the youngest director of a major department that Hopkins had ever had.

Carson attracted international acclaim when he separated Patrick and Benjamin Binder, seven-month-old twins from Germany, on September 4, 1987. Heading a team of seventy doctors, nurses, and support personnel, Carson performed a 22-hour surgery that required lowering the boys' temperature drastically to slow bleeding and then painstakingly untangling and repairing shared blood vessels. While the twins suffered some brain damage, both survived, and Carson was credited with the first successful separation of twins joined in that way.

Carson was awarded the Presidential Medal of Freedom by President George W. Bush.

In 1997, Carson met with similar applause when he traveled to South Central Africa to separate Luka and Joseph Banda, who were conjoined at the tops of their heads. Carson performed a 28-hour operation, which both boys survived with no brain damage.

Carson faced an even greater challenge in 2003, when he was called upon to separate adult conjoined twins, Ladan and Laleh Bijani, 29-year-olds from Iran. Although the chances of success were slim, they explained to Carson that they would rather die than continue to live as they had been. Carson and a team of more than a hundred surgeons and other medical personnel undertook the almost-52-hour procedure with the help of a 3D imaging technique that he had developed, and while both women ultimately died—a virtual certainty given that a major shared blood vessel had fused together—the procedure taught Carson and his colleagues a great deal.

Carson, a survivor of prostate cancer, has written several books about his life and career. These include the autobiography *Gifted Hands* (1996), which was made into a Hollywood film, and the self-help volumes *The Big Picture* (2000), *Think Big* (2006), and *Take the Risk: Learning to Identify, Choose, and Live with Acceptable Risk* (2009). He has been named one of the most important physicians of his era by several media outlets, and the Library of Congress deemed him a "Living Legend" in 2001.

The 2008 recipient of a Presidential Medal of Freedom, the highest civilian honor in the U.S., Carson has, in recent years, become known for his political views, and in 2015 he was a Republican candidate for president. When not involved with politics, Carson is trying to ensure that other young people can follow in his footsteps; since 1994, his Carson Scholars Fund has awarded more than $6 million to high-achieving students hoping to attend college. ●

Words to Understand

savvy
wise, thoughtful, able to use creativity to succeed

unanimously
approved with all present voting in favor

Regina Benjamin

Born:
1956

Nationality:
American

Achievements:
Founder of successful
medical clinic, later
named Surgeon General
of the United States

When President Barack Obama nominated Regina Benjamin to become the 18th Surgeon General of the United States, he called the physician "a relentless promoter of prevention and wellness programs" who "represents what's best about health care in America." Even before being tapped for the high-profile post, Benjamin had earned the admiration of virtually everyone with whom she came in contact. The founder of a nonprofit medical clinic in the poor town of Bayou La Batre, Alabama, she kept it running in the face of financial challenges, hurricane damage, and fire. "It feels good when you help someone, when you make them smile, when you make a difference in their lives, when you stop the hurt," she told an ABC News reporter in 1995. "And you sleep well at night. To me, that's the best reward."

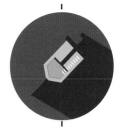

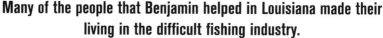

Many of the people that Benjamin helped in Louisiana made their living in the difficult fishing industry.

Benjamin was born on October 26, 1956, in Mobile, Alabama. When she was young, her parents divorced, and she was raised by her mother in the nearby town of Daphne. When money was tight, as it often was, they trekked to the Gulf of Mexico to fish and trap crabs. Benjamin attended nearby Fairhope High School, where she was elected to the student council and honor society.

As her 1975 graduation neared, Benjamin began applying to colleges. Ultimately, she won a scholarship to Xavier University, in New Orleans.

At Xavier, she focused her goals on medicine, rather than law, because of the school's strong pre-med program. (Before entering college, she has said, she had never even seen a black physician.) After earning a B.S. in chemistry in 1979, Benjamin attended the Morehouse School of Medicine and in 1984 she received her M.D. from the University of Alabama at Birmingham. Three years later she completed a family-practice residency at the Medical Center of Central Georgia.

During medical school, Benjamin had received federal financial aid that required her to work for the National Health Services Corps, which sent doctors to poor, underserved communities. Inspired by her time with the organization, in 1990 she opened a one-woman practice that served the residents of Bayou La Batre, a tiny fishing community on Alabama's Gulf Coast, where four out of five people lived below the poverty line. She often used her own funds to buy needed supplies.

"It seems like everyone [here] has a story to tell about this woman who stitches their shark bites, watches over the babies and comes running when accidents at the docks or shipyards injure husbands and sons," a *New York Times* reporter wrote in 1995, after visiting Bayou La Batre. "She makes house calls in a Ford pickup and checks in on shut-ins by telephone. When they cannot pay—which is often— she tells them to pay when they can, what little they can. With envelopes containing single $5 bills, they come by her office: whites, blacks, Vietnamese, Cambodians, Laotians, people who would be turned away by doctors who put proof of insurance ahead of healing."

Benjamin reasoned that she would need to be a **savvy** financial manager in order to keep the clinic running, and she later earned a business degree from Tulane University, traveling more than 100 miles a few times a week to her classes.

In 1995, Benjamin became the first physician under the age of forty and the first African-American woman ever to be elected to the American Medical Association's Board of Trustees. That year she was also the recipient of the Nelson Mandela Award for Health and Human Rights, and similar honors and appointments steadily accrued over the following years.

In 1998, however, the first in a series of disastrous events rocked Bayou La Batre. In mid-September, Hurricane Georges hit the Gulf Coast, causing several deaths and millions of dollars in damages. Benjamin's clinic was left in ruins, but she quickly rebuilt, visiting patients in their homes during the construction process. She was forced to do so again in the wake of Hurricane Katrina, which devastated the area in 2005. Then, in 2006, just as she had recovered from that second catastrophe, a fire tore through the newly reconstructed building. Despite those setbacks, Benjamin remained devoted to her mission and dedicated to the people of Bayou La Batre.

Her work brought her to the attention of government and academic leaders, and in 2009, in a somewhat surprising move, President Obama nominated her as surgeon general. She was confirmed **unanimously** by the US Senate. In her new capacity, Benjamin was charged with spreading the most reliable information on how to improve public health and reduce the risk of illness and injury. She was also assigned to oversee the US Public Health Service Commissioned Corps (USPHS), whose members fill essential public

health leadership roles within federal government agencies.

In explaining why she was honored to accept the post, Benjamin often referenced her own family's history of ill health; her brother had died of HIV, her mother of lung cancer, and her father from the compli-

As Surgeon General, Benjamin often appeared with President Obama to speak on national health issues.

cations of high blood pressure and diabetes.

Responding in part to criticism of her weight, Benjamin embarked on an ambitious agenda to promote wellness and disease prevention. She launched programs that emphasized the importance of nutrition and exercise, as well as programs to encourage breastfeeding and prevent suicide.

In 2013, Benjamin's four-year term expired, and she stepped down to return to her Bayou La Batre clinic. That year the editors of *Reader's Digest* ranked her as one of the "100 Most Trusted People in America." ●

Regina Benjamin:
National health leader

Careers in Medicine

The path to becoming a doctor is a lengthy one. Students can expect to devote more than a decade to the pursuit: four years at an undergraduate college, four years at medical school, and at least three years of in-hospital training, with some specialty programs requiring up to eight years of service as a resident or intern.

Starting in high school and all throughout college, aspiring physicians must build a strong background in math and science—especially in such areas as biology, chemistry, and physics. But because being a good doctor also requires "people" skills like communicating effectively and understanding various cultures, it doesn't pay to ignore humanities courses entirely.

The focus needed during the school year shouldn't stop in the summer. Many experts

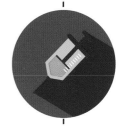

recommend that students volunteer at local hospitals or clinics as a way to meet possible mentors, make their medical-school applications stand out, and, importantly, ensure that a medical career is truly right for them. There are numerous organized offerings available, such as the Robert Wood Johnson Foundation's Summer Medical and Dental Education Program, a free six-week enrichment program for college freshmen and sophomores from racial and ethnic groups that have been historically underrepresented in medicine and dentistry.

Some advisors believe that it is particularly important for minority applicants to carefully consider which medical schools and specialties will best suit them. Most of their fellow students will come from different racial or religious backgrounds—a situation that can easily lead to feelings of isolation and disempowerment. A school may be a better fit if it clearly supports public service, community outreach, and research that focuses on minority health and eliminating disparities in health care.

Preparing for medical school and choosing one are only the initial hurdles, however. Every medical student must face the issue of how to pay for their education. Luckily, there are numerous

A career in medicine is a great way to help people of all ages.

ways to obtain financial aid, with medical schools offering their own scholarships and groups like the National Medical Association being a major source of information on other funding options.

Like Regina Benjamin, students might even subsidize their tuition by joining the National Health Service Corps (NHSC), which offers tax-free loan repayment assistance to support health care providers who choose to take their skills where they're most needed. Graduates can currently earn up to $50,000 toward student loans in exchange for a two-year commitment to practice medicine in a low-income area in dire need of physicians.

Rahn K. Bailey, president of the National Medical Association, once explained to a reporter why it was imperative for students of every stripe to consider medical school, despite the hard work and cost involved. "Society does better with balance all the way around," he said. "And we don't have balance if we have disproportionately twice as many females as males applying to enter the profession, or twice as many from California as from New York, or twice as many people who want to go into surgery as into pediatrics. We need everybody. We need all hands on deck." ●

Text-Dependent Questions

1. Who was responsible for allowing Rebecca Lee Crumpler to complete her medical education?

2. How long did James Cornish remain at Provident to recuperate at the operation by Dr. Williams?

3. By 1953, how many specimens was the Wassermann Lab testing for syphilis each day?

4. Why is plasma useful on the battlefield?

5. What famous doctor inspired Patricia Bath with his humanitarian work?

6. What conditions did Alexa Canady specialize in treating?

7. Why was it useful for Ben Carson to train in Australia?

8. What two catastrophic weather events destroyed Regina Benjamin's clinic?

Suggested Research Projects

1. The "Tuskegee Study of Untreated Syphilis in the Negro Male," which was launched in 1932, marked a shameful period in U.S. medical history. Research the study and think about whether a similar incident would be allowed to happen today.

2. The Red Cross has a long and storied history; research the organization, and write a timeline of major events.

3. The American Institute for the Prevention of Blindness wants to eradicate all preventable blindness around the globe by 2020. What are some of the causes of preventable blindness? How can they be treated?

5. Professor Sebastian Seung runs the Computational Neuroscience Lab at MIT, and you can contribute to his research right from your own computer. Go to eyewire.org and play a game that will help him map human neurons.

6. Ben Carson was sometimes called upon to take part in exceptionally lengthy surgeries. Research some of the longest surgeries on record, choose one and write a paragraph about it.

Find Out More

Websites

www.snma.org
The website of the Student National Medical Association, a group whose goals include serving as a credible and accurate source of information about minority issues in the field of medical education.

www.snma.org/_files/live/SYWTBAD_Update_June_2015.pdf
This link connects to So You Want to Be a Doctor?, a guidebook for aspiring medical students published by the SNMA.

www.aamc.org/students/aspiring
Aspiring Docs is a program created by the Association of American Medical Colleges to provide helpful information and tools for those considering becoming a doctor.

www.studentdoctor.net
The Student Doctor Network is a non-profit educational organization aimed at helping students of all levels learn what they need to know to become doctors.

Books

Taking My Place in Medicine: A Guide for Minority Medical Students. Thousand Oaks, CA: Sage Publications, 2000.
A reference work designed to help minority students thrive personally and academically in medical school, to make a realistic assessment of their strengths and weaknesses.

Tweedy, Damon. *Black Man in a White Coat: A Doctor's Reflections on Race and Medicine*. New York: Picador Publishing, 2015.
This memoir gives an insightful account of the author's experiences grappling with race, bias, and the unique health problems of black Americans.

Series Glossary of Key Terms

botany the study of plant biology

electron a negatively charged particle in an atom

genome all the DNA in an organism, including all the genes

nanometer a measurement of length that is one-billionth of a meter

nanotechnology manipulation of matter on an atomic or molecular scale

patent a set of exclusive rights granted to an inventor for a limited period of time in exchange for detailed public disclosure of an invention

periodic table the arrangement of all the known elements into a table based on increasing atomic number

protein large molecules in the body responsible for the structure and function of all the tissues in an organism

quantum mechanics the scientific principles that describe how matter on a small scale (such as atoms and electrons) behaves

segregated separated, in this case by race

ultraviolet a type of light, usually invisible, that can cause damage to the skin

Index

Photo credits

About the Author

Mari Rich was educated at Lehman College, part of the public City University of New York. As a writer and editor, she has had many years of experience in the fields of university communications and reference publishing, most notably with the highly regarded periodical *Current Biography*, aimed at high school and college readers. She also edited and wrote for *World Authors, Leaders of the Information Age,* and *Nobel Laureates*. Currently, she spends much of her time writing about engineers and engineering.